Bibliographic information published by the German National Library:

The German National Library lists this publication in the National Bibliography; detailed bibliographic data are available on the Internet at http://dnb.dnb.de .

Imprint:

Copyright © 2016 GRIN Verlag, Open Publishing GmbH
Print and binding: Books on Demand GmbH, Norderstedt Germany
ISBN: 9783668334786

This book at GRIN:

http://www.grin.com/en/e-book/342224/using-the-repertory-grid-technique-to-identify-a-good-leader-implications

Malte Eilbracht

Using the Repertory Grid Technique to Identify a Good Leader? Implications for Leading Organisations

GRIN Publishing

GRIN - Your knowledge has value

Since its foundation in 1998, GRIN has specialized in publishing academic texts by students, college teachers and other academics as e-book and printed book. The website www.grin.com is an ideal platform for presenting term papers, final papers, scientific essays, dissertations and specialist books.

Visit us on the internet:

http://www.grin.com/

http://www.facebook.com/grincom

http://www.twitter.com/grin_com

University of Bristol

Faculty of Social Sciences and Law

School of Economics, Finance and Management

UTILISATION OF THE REPERTORY GRID TECHNIQUE IN ODER TO IDENTIFY
THE CHARACTERISTICS OF A GOOD LEADER – SUBSEQUENT DISCUSSION OF
THE FINDINGS REGARDING THEIR IMPLICATIONS FOR LEADING
ORGANISATIONS

Table of Contents

Introduction 1

The Ambiguity of the term 'leadership' 1

The Repertory Grid Technique 3

    Introducing the Repertory Grid Technique 3

    Applying the Repertory Grid Technique 5

    Conclusion of the Repertory Grid Technique 6

Discussion of the findings in context of leading an organisation 7

    Re-thinking the grid 7

    Critique of the re-thought model 9

    Conclusion of the discussion 10

Lists of Tables and Figures

Table 1: "Common Leadership Approaches and their focuses" 1

Table 2: "Trait Approaches" 2

Table 3: "List of Elements" 4

Figure 1: "Original Repertory Grid" 5

Figure 2: "Repertory Grid of Follower 1" 8

Figure 3: "Repertory Matrix" 9

Introduction

The findings of this essay will demonstrate the complex nature of leadership and the ambiguous understanding of the topic. The shortcomings of the Repertory Grid will illustrate why leadership as an academic subject is too complex to be elicited with a single theory, how ambiguity causes bias in the research, and how it causes problems in an organisational context. A subsequent discussion on the Repertory Grid will present a re-thought model as an approach to partly overcome the limitations of the original model. The failure of this approach will be the basis to argue that it might be necessary for organisations to re-think their idea of 'leadership'.

The Ambiguity of the term 'leadership'

This paragraph will indicate the various approaches of Leadership Studies and will argue that its complexity is partly attributable to the vague definition of the term 'leadership'.

It goes without saying that Leadership Theory and the definition of the term 'leadership' highly correlate. The understanding of the term influences and shapes theorists' approaches and vice versa. Therefore, over time a variety of approaches to Leadership Theory have been developed (Bass and Stogdill, 1990; Northouse, 2013). Table 1 gives an infinite overview of common leadership approaches and their focuses.

Table 1: "Common Leadership Approaches and their focuses"

Theory / Approach	Focus
Trait Approach	Traits of the Leader
Skills Approach	Skills of the Leader
Style Approach	Behaviour or Action of the Leader
Situational Approach	Leader's capability to adapt to a given situation
Contingency Theory	Matching the right leader to the right setting
Path-Goal Theory	Employee satisfaction and motivation
Leader-Member Exchange Theory	Dyadic relationship between leader and follower
Transformational / Transactional Leadership	The charismatic and affective elements of leadership
Servant Leadership	Leader's ability to empowerment and nurture followers
Team Leadership	Leader's ability to ensure the team's effectiveness

Source: Bass and Stogdill, 1990; Northouse, 2013

The approaches listed in Table 1 indicate, that they cannot be based on the same definition of 'leadership', as some theories focus on a set of characteristics, while others see leadership as a process between leader and followers. Northouse (2013) claims that 21st Century's scholars agree on the impossibility to find a standard definition of 'leadership'. The vague definition of the term causes an incoherence in the understanding of leadership, which in turn causes complexity in the academic field. Table 1 gave an overview of the different approaches to Leadership Theory, whereas Table 2 will provide an overview of the divergence within the findings of one[1] of these approaches.

Table 2: "Trait Approaches"

Stogdill (1948)	Mann (1959)	Stogdill (1974)	Lord, DeVader, Alliger (1986)	Kirkpatrick, Locke (1991)	Zaccaro, Kemp, Bader (2004)
Intelligence	Intelligence	Achievement	Intelligence	Drive	Cognitive abilities
Alertness	Masculinity	Persistence	Masculinity	Motivation	Extraversion
Insight	Adjustment	Insight	Dominance	Integrity	Conscientiousness
Responsibility	Dominance	Initiative		Confidence	Emotional stability
Initiative	Extraversion	Self-confidence		Cognitive ability	Openness
Persistence	Conservatism	Responsibility		Task knowledge	Agreeableness
Self-confidence		Cooperativeness			Motivation
Sociability		Tolerance			Social intelligence
		Influence			Self-monitoring
		Sociability			Emotional intelligence
					Problem solving

Source: Northouse 2013 p.23

Table 2 lists the results of six decades in research of leadership traits. The divergence in the findings is partly attributable to the research method, but also reflects the equivocal understanding of the term 'leadership' by the research subjects. Northouse (2013) critics that "[…] over the past 100 years, the findings from these studies have been ambiguous and uncertain at times." (Northouse, 2013, p.30). Rost and Burns (1991) argue a similar way: "The […] problem with leadership studies as an academic discipline […] is that neither the scholars nor the practitioners have been able to define leadership with precision, accuracy, and conciseness […]." (Rost and Burns, 1991, p. 6.). Following the above-given argumentation on the ambiguity of leadership as well as the work of Rost and Bruns (1991) and Northouse (2013), it shall be noted:

Finding 1: 'leadership' is an ambiguous term, which causes complexity and problems in leadership studies.

---

[1] As an example this essay will focus on the trait approach, but similar effects, of divergent findings caused by the vague definition of the term 'leadership', can be found in other approaches as well (Bass and Stogdill, 1990; Rost and Burns 1991; Northouse, 2013)

The Repertory Grid Technique

This paragraph will introduce the Repertory Grid Technique and argue that the method is not useful to identify generalities of leadership. While applying the technique, it will be demonstrated that findings will be multiple biased and therefore this paragraph will not include any characteristics of leadership found by the author.

Introducing the Repertory Grid Technique

The Repertory Grid Technique is rooted in the work of psychologist G.A. Kelly. Kelly (1955, 1963) argues that people create their personal system of constructs with which they experience their reality. In his words: "Man looks at his world through transparent patterns or templates which he creates and then attempts to fit over the realities of which the world is composed." (Kelly, 1963, pp. 8-9). To illustrate the technique of the grid, this essay refers to a simplified view[2] of constructs as a person's bi-polar view on the characteristics of a family of elements (Kelly 1955, 1966; Ryle, 1975; Fransella and Bannister, 1977). An element can theoretically be any entity, which fulfils the following two criteria. The element must "represent the domain in which construing is to be investigated" (Beail, 1985, p. 3). In other words, if 'leadership' is the domain of investigation, the elements of the grid should be widely accepted leaders, rather than using a friend or family member as an element of investigation. Secondly, the elements should provide repeatable outcomes (Mitsos, 1958). In other words, if the characteristics of a leader are the domain of investigation, 'Angela Merkel' should be the element, rather than 'German Chancellor', as the element 'German Chancellor' can change over time, whereas the element 'Angela Merkel' is more consistent. Table 3 lists the elements chosen by the author to carry out a grid exercise on leadership.

---

[2] For further details on the psychologists idea of constructs and the methods to identify those please refer to Kelly (1955 , 1963), Ryle (1975) or Fransella and Bannister, (1977)

Table 3: "List of Elements"

Element	Short Discerptions
Angela Merkel	German Chancellor and important figure in the European Union
Jack Ma	Executive Chairman of Alibaba Group – the world's largest online business
Joe Dunford	Highly decorated U.S. General and leader of the NATO's coalition in Afghanistan
Geoffrey Canada	CEO of the 'Harlem Children's Zone' – a project giving education as well as social and medical help to children in Harlem
Kim Jong-un	Supreme leader of the Democratic People's Republic of Korea

At this stage, it can be argued that the selected elements fulfil the above-mentioned criteria of representing the domain 'leadership' and will provide repeatable outcomes. Nevertheless, it must be criticised that the elements are randomly chosen and that the sample size of five cannot supply significant data regarding the amount of elements in the domain 'leadership', which theoretically could have been selected. For later argumentation of this essay, it shall be noted:

Finding 2: The choice of elements is biased by the person constructing the repertory grid and therefore influences the outcome of the research.

To further exercise the repertory grid, elicitation of the constructs is required. As mentioned above, this essay refers to the view of constructs as a person's bi-polar view on the characteristics of a family of elements. Kelly (1955) outlines six different ways to build a construct. For the cause of the grid exercise in this essay, the author refers to the 'Sequential Form' described by Fransella and Bannister (1977), referencing the work of Kelly (1955)[3]. Thereby, every combination of three elements is presented, and it is "asked to specify some important way in which two of them are alike and thereby different from the third" (Fransella and Bannister, 1977, p.14). Using this way of elicitation, it has to be critically evaluated what the meaning of an 'important way' is. Applying the method to the triad Angela Merkel, Jack Ma, Kim Jong-un, it can be found that two elements are 'black haired', while one is 'not black haired'. This construct is likely to be rejected by researchers, whereas 'male' – 'female' is an arguable construct. The findings of Mann (1959) as well as the work of Lord, DeVader and Alliger (1986), as shown in Table 2, present 'masculinity' as a leadership trait. From a feminist perspective, the leadership qualities are not connected to that person's sex (Dawley, Hoffman & Smith, 2004). This example illustrates that, due to an individual's decision of what is 'important' and what is not, the outcome

---

[3] A description of the method can be found in (Fransella and Bannister 1977, pp. 11 - 22). For further understanding of the nature of personal constructs refer to (Kelly, 1963, pp. 105- 183)

of the grid is biased. Another problem illustrated by this example, is the dichotomous articulation of the scale (Millis and Niemeier, 1990; Riemann, 1990). The bi-polar scale of the first construct was set to be 'black haired' – 'not black haired'. It could also be thought of to be 'black haired' – 'blond haired', which, regardless of its rejection, would bias the outcome of the grid (Bonarius et al., 1984). The same applies to 'male' – 'female' instead of 'male' – 'not male' or 'female' – 'not female'. This example presents the shortcomings of the elicitation of the constructs. Therefore, it should be noted.

Finding 3: The elicitation of constructs is double biased by the person creating the Repertory Grid, as he or she decides what is 'important' and how the scale is labelled

Applying the Repertory Grid Technique

As the *Findings 1, 2 and 3* already demonstrate the bias and subjectivity involved in the construction of the grid. At this stage, it should be clear to the reader that the following grid would only represent the author's biased opinion on 'important' leadership characteristics of the chosen elements. Hence, they will not be outlined in this essay. Still, as an illustration of the method, the grid shall be constructed as following: Out of the variety of different grids, which are in use (Fransella and Bannister, 1977), this essay refers to the Rating-Grid described by Hjelle and Ziegler (1976). As mentioned above, the constructs will be elicited using the 'Sequential Form' on the elements listed in Table 3. The constructs are rated for each leader on a scale of 1 to 10.

Figure 1: "Original Repertory Grid"

	Angela Merkel	Jack Ma	Joe Dunford	Geoffrey Canada	Kim Jong-un
Construct 1	10	8	5	4	1
Construct 2	2	4	6	8	4
Construct 3	7	6	8	9	6
Construct 4	8	9	7	3	5
Construct 5	6	3	8	4	10
Construct 6	8	6	8	8	7

Source: Adaption of (Hjelle and Ziegler, 1976) as found in (Fransella and Bannister, 1977, p. 41)

To present the outcome of the grid correctly, it must be read in a way like this: The Author identified Angela Merkel, Jack Ma, Joe Dunford, Geoffrey Canada and Kim Jong-un as leaders and found constructs 1 - 6 to be vital characteristics of leadership. He thinks Angela Merkel is to be rated 10 out of 10 on the construct 1, on a scale, which he primarily defined himself.

Whether one agrees with the author's opinion or not, the scientific value of this grid, to gain insight into the studies of leadership, has to be dined. Thus, it shall be noted:

Finding 4: In consideration of the findings 1, 2 and 3 it can be concluded that the repertory grid is not useful to identify generalities of leadership

Conclusion of the Repertory Grid Technique

It was found that the grid is not suitable to give general insight into the understanding of leadership. The argumentation is based on the method's inherent bias as highlighted in the *findings 1, 2 and 3*. In more detailed words, while selecting the 'elements' of the grid, a person can only refer to his/her knowledge base. To be selected as an 'element', a 'leader' must be known and be acknowledged by the researcher. The same logic applies to the 'constructs'. To be listed in the grid, characteristics must be identified as leadership characteristics[4] beforehand. This leads to a paradox. The scholar must know who a leader is and what characteristics a leader has <u>before</u> the research on leadership can take place. Another shortcoming of the method is the definition of the scale of the constructs. To implement a scale into a grid it must be bi-polar. Therefore, the method does not allow the inclusion of complex constructs in an appropriate way. A further problem related to the definition of the scale is its articulation. Scales are bounded by the precession and language[5] of the researcher. Finally, due to its 2-dimensional format, the grid implies that constructs are static. A leader has or has not a certain characteristic, but it is not possible to represent leadership as something dynamic. - Does the leader have the characteristic in every situation and show it equally to every follower? - As there is no determining variable in the grid, ideas such as the Situational Approach or Leader-Member Exchange Theory are not representable.

---

[4] Or traits / skills / behaviour
[5] A translated grid is likely to come up with different findings as the translated scales might have slightly different meanings in the source language.

Discussion of the findings in context of leading an organisation

The paragraph on the Repertory Grid stressed the shortcomings of the model. It needs to be understood that those shortcoming are also a reflection of the topic. The grid itself is neither good nor bad, it is either more or less applicable. In this case, the grid did not appeal to the equivocal character of leadership. The following discussion will use the findings of this essay to develop a new and more applicable technique, which could be used in an organisational context and present a different way to think about leadership.

Re-thinking the grid

It was shown that the Repertory Grid Technique is influenced by the underlying assumptions and opinions on leadership by the constructing person. It was argued, that it therefore is not useful to gain scientific insights in the studies of leadership but there might be a case where this inherent bias is appreciated. A re-thought model could lead to an applicable tool for 'leadership' in an organisational context. This approach is based on the *findings 1— 4* and the view of leadership as a role in a bureaucratic structure (Weber, 1968). In large organisation bureaucracy structures, the office hierarchy is a "clearly established system of super- and subordination (Weber, 1968, p. 957). Managers, Team Leaders or CEO's are replaceable within an organisation. If they are replaced, their managerial responsibility becomes the obligation of the new 'leader' (Weber, 1968). In most companies, candidates are selected by the Human Resource Department. At the end of the application process, the selected candidate takes over the role of the leader for a specific group of followers. The role of 'leader' and 'follower' is set by the bureaucratic structures and the set-up of the organisation. The work of the Human Resource Department should be, to maximise the fit between the 'leader' and the 'follower'. In this case the inherent bias of the Repertory Grid can help with the task, as the grid is useful to identify a person distinct view on a topic (Warren, 1998; Chiari and Nuzzo, 2003; Butt, 2004, 2005). What above was criticised as a 'bias' in identifying generalities of leadership is now labelled a person's 'specific view' on leadership, and is the focus of the elicitation. A company could apply the repertory grid as follows:

Given the situation of replacing a line manager, subordinate staff are asked to identify essential characteristics, skills, traits, and behaviours of a direct supervisor. If the job candidates for the 'leader' position are already known, it can be thought of using Kelly's (1955) approach by asking "to specify some important way in which two of them are alike and thereby different from the third" (Fransella and Bannister, 1977, p.14). Those characteristics are used as the constructs of the grid, while the elements are the job candidates for the 'leader' position. After the candidates have been rated, the outcome will appear in the following manner.

Figure 2: "Repertory Grid of Follower 1"

Follower 1	Candidate 1	Candidate 2	Candidate 3	Candidate 4	Candidate 5
Construct 1	8	7	8	7	3
Construct 2	8	8	8	8	8
Construct 3	7	7	8	7	6
Construct 4	8	6	10	10	1
Construct 5	6	7	8	9	6
Construct 6	7	8	8	8	2
Construct 7	8	8	9	8	10
Construct 8	8	7	8	7	1
Construct 9					
Construct 10					
Construct 11					
SCORE	75%	73%	84%	80%	46%

The Repertory Grid now reflects the specific view of 'Follower 1' on eight important characteristics, skills, traits or behaviours a direct supervisor should have. It also includes the ranking of the five possible candidates for the vacancy. It can be found that 'Candidate 3' will satisfy the expectations of 'Follower 1' the best. Applying this systematic to all subordinates, the repertory grid becomes 3-dimensional, as it adds the dimension of the followers.

Figure 3: "Repertory Matrix"

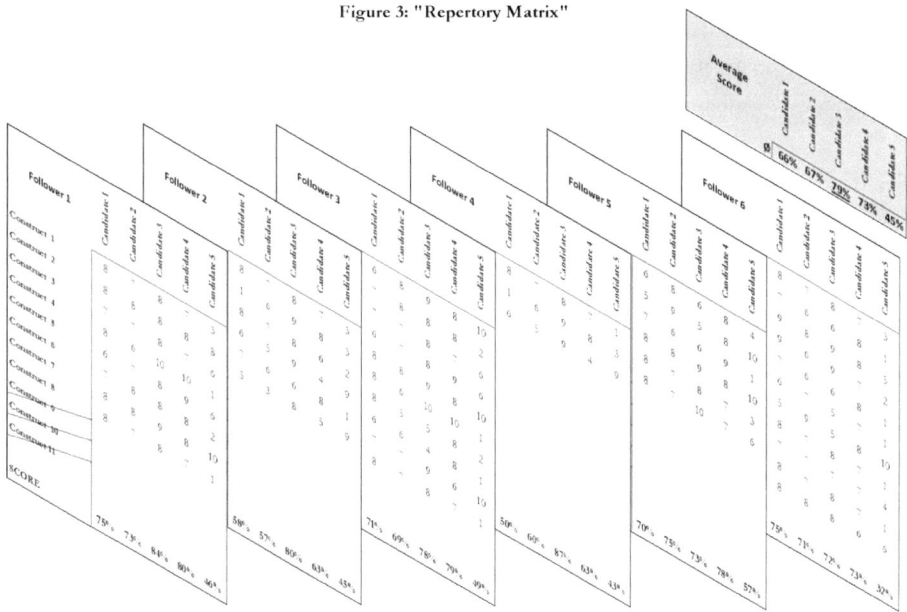

This approach allows the Human Resource Department to identify the team's unique view on leadership and their expectations towards a new line manager. Calculating the average score, as shown in the grey box, it is possible to find the best 'leader' for a particular team, while equally representing every team member's expectations. Choosing the candidate with the highest average score would maximize the fit between 'leader' and 'follower' in an organisational context, where bureaucratic structures regulate both parties' roles.

Critique of the re-thought model

The new model partly overcomes some of the initial shortcomings. While allowing the followers do define the criteria of the leader, the model gives credit to elements of various approaches. The role of the followers and their satisfaction is acknowledged. This idea is also represented in the Path-Goal-Theory (House, 1996; Jermier, 1996). The new model also acknowledges that organisations in different situations might need a different type of leadership as it implies that the followers would adjust their constructs regarding the situation they find themselves in. Similar ideas can be found in the Situational Approach, as well as in the Contingency Theory

(Donaldson, 2001). A shortcoming of the model, which couldn't be overcome, is the rating of the construct. It implies that the Human Resource Department or the team is able to rate the candidates on the elicited constructs. In other words all candidates, their characters, skills, traits and behaviours must be well known, to give a fair ranking. This idea contradicts with the business environment where it is common to source staff outside of the company. Hence, the re-thought model might overcome some of the identified shortcomings of the original grid, but still cannot be used in an organisational context.

Conclusion of the discussion

This paper followed the approach to use the repertory grid to identify the characteristics of Leadership. Throughout the essay, it was stressed on different levels that the character of the method doesn't appeal the nature of the topic. It was demonstrated that 'leadership' has no common definition, it is ambiguous, and therefore, a phenomena which is experienced differently. Using the repertory grid, implies the idea that 'leadership' has governing rules or attributes and it is manageable in an organisational context. Those contrasting findings cause a problem. How can an organisation effectively be lead, if all its members might have a different understanding of leadership? The re-thought model showed that, even if it would be possible to identify a team's understanding of leadership, it is problematic to match the right person to the role. Therefore, it is also not applicable. The complexity of the topic, lead to the failure of the grid. And the complexity of the topic also causes the development of many different approaches of leadership studies. As there can be found evidence for every approach, there is also critic for every model. Therefore, it can be concluded that the 'leadership' is a too complex topic to be explained in a universal theory. Following the author's opinion, it might be necessary for organisations to broaden their understanding of leadership, and apply a more abstract view. The findings of this essay imply that there are a multitude of understandings on leadership, which are to a certain degree coherent. Academic approaches try to identify the coherent element to give a definition of leadership, but it was shown that over a century of research failed to give a common definition. Organisations should acknowledge the polymorph character of 'leadership', which comes in various forms and is shaped through various factors. The study of leadership might help to understand some of the mechanism, but is unable explain it as a whole.

References

Bass, B. and Stogdill, R. M. (1990). *Bass & Stogdill's handbook of leadership*: Theory, Research and Managerial Applications. New York: Free Press.

Beail, N. (1985). *Repertory grid technique and personal constructs*. London: Croom Helm.

Bonarius, H., Van Heck, G., & Smid, N. (Eds.). (1984). *Personality psychology in Europe: Theoretical and empirical developments*. Lisse: Swets & Zeitlinger.

Butt, T. W. (2004). *Understanding, explanation, and personal constructs*. Personal Construct Theory & Practice, 1, 1, pp. 21 – 27.

Butt, T. W. (2005). *Personal construct theory, phenomenology and pragmatism*. History and Philosophy of Psychology, 7, 1, pp. 223 – 235.

Chiari, G., & Nuzzo, M. L. (2003). *Kelly's philosophy of constructive alternativism*. In F. Fransella (Ed.), *International handbook of personal construct psychology*. pp.41 – 49. Chichester: Wiley.

Dawley, D., Hoffman, J.J., & Smith, A.R. (2004) *Leader succession: does gender matter?*, Leadership & Organization Development Journal, 25, 8, pp. 678 – 690.

Donaldson, L. (2001). *The contingency theory of organizations*. Thousand Oaks, Calif.: Sage Publications.

Hjelle, L.A. and Ziegler, D.J. (1976). *Personality Theories: Basic Assumptions, Research, and Applications*. McGraw-Hill, New York.

House, R.J. (1996). *Path-goal theory of leadership: Lessons, legacy, and a reformulated theory*. The Leadership Quarterly, 1996, 7, 3, pp. 323 – 352

Jermier, J.M. (1996). *The path-goal theory of leadership: A subtextual analysis*. The Leadership Quarterly, 1996, 7, 3, pp.311 – 316

Fransella, F. and Bannister, D. (1977). *A manual for repertory grid technique*. London: Academic Press.

Kelly, G. (1955). *The psychology of personal constructs*. New York: W.W. Norton.

Kelly, G. (1963). *A theory of personality*. New York: W.W. Norton.

Kirkpatrick, S.A., & Locke, E.A. (1991). *Leadership: Do traits matter?* The Executive, 5, 48 – 60.

Lord, R.G., DeVader, C.L., & Alliger, G.M. (1986). *A meta-analysis of the relation between personality traits and leadership perceptions: An application of validity generalization procedures*. Journal of Applied Psychology, 71, 402 – 410.

Mann, R.D. (1959). *A review of the relationship between personality and performance in small groups*. Psychological Bulletin, 56, 241 – 270.

Millis, K. K., & Neimeyer, R. A. (1990). *A test of the dichotomy corollary: propositions versus constructs as basic cognitive units*. International Journal of Personal Construct Psychology, 3, pp. 167 -181.

Mitsos, S.B. (1958). *Representative elements in role construct technique.* Journal of Consulting Psychology, 22, 311-313.

Northouse, P. (2013). *Leadership.* Thousand Oaks: SAGE.

Riemann, R. (1990). *The bipolarity of personal constructs.* International Journal of Construct Psychology, 3, pp. 149 – 165.

Ryle, A. (1975). *Frames and cages: The Repertory Grid Approach to Human Understanding.* London: Published for Sussex University Press by Chatto and Windus.

Rost, J. and Burns, J. (1991). *Leadership for the twenty-first century.* New York: Praeger.

Stogdill R. M. (1948). *Personal factor associated with leadership: A survey of the literature.* Journal of Psychology, 25, 35-71.

Stogdill R. M. (1974). *Handbook of leadership: A survey of theory and research.* New York: Free Press.

Warren, W. (1998). *Philosophical dimensions of personal construct psychology.* London: Routledge.

Weber, M. (1968). *Economy and society.* New York: Bedminster Press.

Zaccaro, S. J., Kemp, C., & Bader, P. (2004). *Leader traits and attributes.* In J. Antonakis, A.T. Cianciolo, & R. J. Sternberg (Eds.), *The nature of leadership*, pp. 101 – 124. Thousand Oaks, CA: Sage.